Ashes

poems by

Mike Matthews

Finishing Line Press
Georgetown, Kentucky

Ashes

for Dad

Copyright © 2022 by Mike Matthews
ISBN 978-1-64662-910-7 First Edition
All rights reserved under International and Pan-American Copyright Conventions. No part of this book may be reproduced in any manner whatsoever without written permission from the publisher, except in the case of brief quotations embodied in critical articles and reviews.

ACKNOWLEDGMENTS

Thank you to all who
called to the void for this book
and guided my pen.

Thank you to the online literary journal, *iddie*, first edition, for publishing my poem, "Our Bones," in 2007.

Publisher: Leah Huete de Maines
Editor: Christen Kincaid
Cover Art: Mike Matthews; Digital Medium, *Ash*
Author Photo: Mike Matthews
Cover Design: Elizabeth Maines McCleavy

Order online: www.finishinglinepress.com
also available on amazon.com

Author inquiries and mail orders:
Finishing Line Press
PO Box 1626
Georgetown, Kentucky 40324
USA

Table of Contents

Start With Nothing 1
Charged with Seeing 2
Notes 3
All of the Ordinary Hours 4
I Keep Looking 5
A Moment 6
A Man and His Ham and Eggs 7
Agita 8
A Man in the Road on a Blind Curve 9
I Could Go on, But… 10
A Metonym in a Day 11
White Ashes 12
Our Lives in Boxes 13
Saké Conversation 14
Today and Tomorrow 15
Empty Chairs 16
Ashes 18
Fleck of Dust 19
Water and Air 20
Natural Pain 21
The Last Gaping Yawn 22
Glass Thin Denial 23
Black Glass 24
Broken Bottles 25
From Now Until 26
Dead Tree and Rotting Mobile Home 27
The Dry, Red Desert 28
Our Bones 29
The Book of Waves 30
Coverless Night 32
Cremated 33
Grief and Seeking 35

Start with Nothing

Start with nothing. Turn on the lamp:
Cluttered paper, one tarnished ear ring,
wet socks, thick black leaves outside, the cold.

Start in the present under a lamp—
nothing that arrives from nowhere,
with the present that is memory from the future:
a broken toy rubber robot with a torn arm,
empty candy wrapper, untied paper clips.

Resurrect some memory: my orange bike
with the banana seat, to see my father.
I stopped at a water fountain,
the only decision I could make for myself: to drink.
The bike burned orange, flame-orange.

Start with the lamp under an empty midnight.
Dig into a dream from nowhere two days late—
Not the dream practiced during the drive to work
that breaks between words about lost moments
without touching, without a touch—

Start in a dream where a desk has little room for elbows.
Let chores rain from the lamp's bulb
and pool in intuitive falling, a late bill, midnight
wrapped around a black tree stump.

Start with crumpled receipts, worn out clothes,
stained glasses of empty wine under lamplight
tangled with orange memories.

End with some middle between the lamp and the desk—
Start from nothing and end stacked against the wake of days.

Charged with Seeing

The unseen makers of stillness,
ghosts whose breath
skims my frayed sleeves,
charge me with the madness of seeing.

They whisper songs of the stillest winds.

I traipse in between breaths,
mad to be in time.

Their words break silence
                            always breaking.

Steady in the fast from eating time,
I defend my identity,
but the dues I owe come due.

Their whispers touch the hands of tower clocks
and show that minutes never move.
All along, their moving has been of my hands pushing,
                                                pushing.
Under the sum-line,
where the columns of added seconds merge,
the still bells of the stillest time still chime.

Notes

I have left notes on the kitchen counter for me to find
of lists of tasks and phone numbers I would not retain
while I disappeared in sleep.

Should I find the notes and spill coffee on them,
blurring the proof that I had existed,
sometime before or sometime during midnight,
I could have the proof I need that I was absent
for a moment, asleep in the waves
of some ether sea dream of some lost evening
never knowing or not knowing of myself.

As if I'd telegrammed my future
and received the message from my past,
the simultaneity sought by physicists,
the present morning reassembles me
from the night before and the night before,
and strings all the nights together
with cryptic lines of things to remember
and things to do that remind me
that I am on a paper road
that yellows at night and burns
on the edges of a day.

All of the Ordinary Hours

All of the ordinary hours are bullets of quick intensities,
compressed, disguised by one another and each other's rapid vibrations.

They are masks of the ordinary—as if the cup I washed today
becomes the same one I poured coffee into through a filter
in the morning the day before, and since there is a multiplication,
there pretends to be continuation: one cup one day, same cup the next.

If, though, each breath were a drop of water in a stream
slowed enough that each were distinguishable, some silver,
some red, some clear, one amber or yellow, the hours strung together
by the separate droplets, like moments in a stream revealed by light
flashing in a strobe and overwhelming the richness of senses,
would double the richness of a unique drop to capture until the next.

One drop's powerful perfection sings a note at once extraordinary,
and the sheering, sharp surprise at such awakening to that which seemed
to have blended with that which seemed to have been overlooked
could knock the sturdiest to their knees and cause a mysterious
weeping at the loss of veiled vision, and the shock could shake
the solid wall of foregone conclusions by the intensity
of brilliance of each moment revealed.

I Keep Looking

I am looking for something,
so I know I won't find it.

I have listened by looking

        at the dragonflies,
        at the dust blown into my eyes
        and down my throat
        by every coming storm,
        at the bricks broken everywhere
        to replace old shops with new towers,
        at the families riding one electric scooter,
        at the tired, concentrating bus drivers,
        at the eyes that stare at me,
        the foreigner, the lǎo wài,
        at the monks with stern faces
        after they chant, who spot me
        listening cross-legged
        on the step of the old temple,
        at the trash and dog crap
        on the brick sidewalks,
        at the resigned face of the dying man
        whose eyes long deeply to leave
        the long hours in his last bed
        where nothing happens
        and no one visits.

I listen, look, and I still hide what I seek.

A Moment

A moment stole me from my busy evening.
The air seemed yellow and fresh,
not like the summers from yesterday afternoon.

The hill, Hog Mountain,
behind our humble duplex apartment
lay covered with green juniper
and patches of caliche—a living stillness.

Bugs floated over the yuccas, the sage bushes,
the power lines, the vacant lot
and reflected the easy light
like puffs of yellow stardust.

Like loose strings from a strange instrument,
spider silk casually sailed across the sky
and through the shallow clouds of insects
tying the sky to the leaves, gentle and fine.

A Man and His Ham and Eggs

A pertinent point what leaked off his lower lip,
pronunciation like a swollen cotton ball,
tone like grey weather before morning clock-in.
Those eggs on his plate ran from cracks in their shells,
and his ham slice glowed like teen-pink fingernails.

I kept my coffee black enough for it to get cold,
but the refills slopped over the rim again, warm like tap-water.
He crooned a mumbled, shallow-end observation
followed by an assertion disguised as a stone.

Someone knocked a saucer from a table
cracking like a snapped cube of air
and inviting an instantly opened and instantly closed exit.

He'd chewed a fork full of ham, as if allowing his truth
to permeate a universal consciousness,
or to awaken the unaware to their own history of ignorance.
The topic could've been anything, as undercooked as his eggs:
elections, marriage, immigration, women, foreign policy, hash browns.

Agita

Agita, in her pink, dirt-fluffy slippers,
late morning, past all else's second cups,
her coffee from a can, red most likely,
leaves her front door for a short, bed-hair walk
to the morning paper, never dewed wet,
in her aqua-blue cloth robe
like she's always a swimming pool.

She stayed up late, again, calling to awaken
her friend who can never say that she needs to sleep
or that she has to take her young children to school,
who martyrs her workday for Agita another night.
Her heart is addicted to caffeine so she can keep her job,
though Agita sleeps in—where does Agita's money come from,
         her friend wonders?

Agita only sees the words, the newsprint, the crosswords,
not the serious war in the cradle of civilization,
not the waning supply of fresh water,
but the prophetic generalities of horoscopes,
and occasionally the throaty chuckle of a simple comic strip
while her last cold slag of coffee grows a cream film,
and she wonders why her hours bleed away
like random dreams that fade under the sun's brilliant heat
filtered through yellow curtains and outshining
the kitchen bulb, though no one, not even Agita,
         would ever cut the light.

A Man in the Road on a Blind Curve

He sought a pinch of understanding,
swaggering in the lanes of a Saturday's blind curve,
hands held up to stop a truck, to slow the day,
like thick paddles on the end of his stout arms.

He turned his palm up and tilted his head,
the request of his life, not for a coin.
Did he need a ride, a drink, an answer?

He half raised a side of his mouth and half squinted
as if to say, "C'mon, c'mon, c'mon."
Surely he needed someone to stop and tell him
that he was ok or that he would not need to step
along the Saturday road's lanes to seek
the answers to his begging questions
that quietly erode within the static of his desperate day.

I Could Go On…But,

The line between morning and sleep blurs,
motionless next to the window.
A flake of notion flickers.
I fumble in my unwashed clothes.

Together, the clock of place and step, look and breathe
winds through routine of downtown.
Those faces again and those hobbling souls
fill my pocket with trinkets I forget to throw away.

The chatter: A man empties his coffee in sprinkles;
a woman grips her skirt against cold gusts.
She locks her eyes in a concrete flower.

The shadows:
Tunes from cars strewn by drivers with no faces.

Pecking pigeons pinhole their shadows,
here, where a child throws gum,
and there, where a man yells to his wife,
and here where a bike locks to rust on the lamppost.

These rows of yesterdays grow like shadows
stretching toward the opposite horizons
of grey mornings and chalky sunsets.

A Metonym in a Day

When the day retracts its blossoms,
folding its petals into itself,
reaching its stillest moment
at the frozen second of midnight,

kitchens that were opened close,
and conversations move from history to future
where all the unplanned phrases and responses settle
on inactive linoleum that no longer shines.
Then the night moves like tumblers
escaping canyon walls to splash in shallow rivers.

Bosses finish delivering their glowing compliments
with smiles to the walk-in-closet offices
with workers stuck between the clutter of scratch paper,
the dust from dissolving yellowed handbooks,
and broken air-conditioners breathing like humid fists—

Could anyone in any room inside any minute
along the downslope slide of time
record the metonyms of these moments?

The twitching smiles in florescent hallways,
the dirt under uncut fingernails
that clack on keys of chrome computers,
the ragged topknots over sleep deprived, unshaven faces
dark and lined with the paths of disillusion
squeezed between eyebrows like relief tattoos
of a society in a darkened mind—

The eyes and the eyes and the eyes
and the days stick on thoughts
like debris hanging in barren trees
                            after a terrible flood.

White Ashes

What did Dad see when he looked at the horizon
filled with gulf water and small breaking waves?

When did he look at the sea and say, "That's where
I want to go, to let my ashes sift into salt and sand"?

What kind of freedom did the coast give him
from his struggle with his body
born with holes in its heart
that he could never breathe enough
to run like the boundless wind and waves?

Fishers on the pier showed us their one big fish
curled in a cooler and wrapped with rubber bands.
A slow barge left the wide mouth of the river
leaving the boundary of the shore for the sea.
Grackles shuttled on the bank and gurgled.
No seagulls swarmed over the few dead fish.

We found a charred log on the shore
that burned black in a distant fire.

His brass urn shined in the bright October sun.
The white smoke from the incense
smelled like the sweet calm of a temple,
and the small flames on the candles
slowly descended through the words,
Happiness, Health, Forever.

We poured his ashes in the ocean
where the Colorado River meets the Gulf of Mexico,
where the waves felt like fists
when they broke against our chests.

Dad's caliche white ashes
sifted into the sandy brown water
where they spread together
with the endless breathing waves
                            forever indistinguishable.

Our Lives in Boxes

The value of a moment,
the achievements,
ID cards with our second
attempts to smile,
Father's Day cards from sons,
report cards from elementary schools,
letters from parents,
important files in case, just in case,
drawings from kindergarten,
cartoon strips from childhood,
pictures of weddings,
pictures of places,
pictures, pictures, pictures,
old address books
with phone numbers decades old,
transcripts and degrees,
state flag refrigerator magnets,
paperclips and old laptops,
RCA and VHS recorders
all encased just in case
we need to use them,
we need to remember them,
we need to make ourselves from them,
in case we forget who we are,
what makes us happy,
what we worked so long to develop,
encased in silverfish-jagged,
spider ridden boxes
passed to the sons and daughters
to decide what to set free,
to untangle the spirit from the files,
to sever the invisible need,
encased, just in case,
we need to remember

the work we do for our mothers,
the work we do for our fathers.

Saké Conversation

I raised the ancient, hand-sized blue bowl to my lips,
three hundred years of kisses.

Ray said,
      "To come back from visiting the dead,
      jolted back into my mind—
      out there had nothing to do with being here.
      I spoke with my mother
      who was surrounded by radiance.
      The immense sadness of returning."

A lamp glowed, his face silhouetted.
Friday evening candles burned—
broken bread and a goblet of red wine.

He said,
      "I will lay myself in a gorge in Colorado
      where the first snows of October
      will pile onto my body.

      A glacier will harden and slide
      like a slow ice-blade tearing my flesh,
      carrying the pieces to the plains,
      the mountains green and wet, soft
      with pine needles and treetop wind.

      The weight of the ice will embed
      my body into the soil.
      I will flow in pieces,
      and the ice will melt,
      erosion and me in mutual consciousness
      resting on the banks,
      tangled in the roots of pine and cottonwood."

Saké slid over the back of my tongue—
      warm rain softly buttered.

Today and Tomorrow

Surely tomorrow is carved from today.
Its wood-dust from the fine tools and sandpaper
already swept into neat piles so tomorrow's woodblock
should shine, polished smooth.

One could count on the same pair of shoes tied today
to knot the laces of tomorrow, surely—
or arrive at new and simple glances from admiring eyes
to reassure one's physical existence,
to catch that moment that holds today and carries it
to tomorrow's metonymic moment,
to apply it to a deduced future
that slips its finger along
the stained and polished curves
of a darkstained, darkwood sculpture of tomorrow,
wishful, graceful, and deciduous.

Empty Chairs

I lift memories from these empty chairs
of friends who have sat there, decade after decade,
all of time melded and simultaneous.

Two times before, I was there. Once, I am not.
But before is still now, and time is a sphere
with spontaneous contours.

I sip from my teacup
together with what is now and what is past,
when friends are poets in empty chairs.

Hovering behind my shoulders, they are stuck in another decade,
living that life again and again while I live this one.
Only this time I am the one at the table.

Another time through this same line, and my tea is not black.
Instead, someone sits across from me, and we spill coffee.
Or, outside it rains.

Who are the two missing people
I know from the mesas of New Mexico
or from the stone buildings in Northern Europe?
Their shadows fill these chairs.

I die, I sit, and I write.
I write, I sip, and I die.
How many times have we passed this moment?

Last time, two poets sit here.
Last time, I smoke, and the poet on my left
lives in Ireland.

Simultaneous decades, simultaneous centuries:
I sit, write, and live as a nomad,
wandering the icy peeks of Norway.

Time does not clip its umbilical.
Linearity blinds me.

Two empty chairs that are never filled
with two poets I don't meet
who live now sit centuries ago
sipping tea on a mountain, staring at an empty chair.

Ashes

All of those concerns
mask a motivation
to adjust, to prepare, to prevent,
to keep from forgetting
so much importance.

Ashes

The story of the self
fits in the little notes in a wallet,
a photo and a café card,
loose change that drives minutes.

Ashes

The lenses in a pair of glasses,
a last pair of sandals,
and a red shirt barely
keep a ghost's shape
folded in the moment
of empty jeans and dandruff.

Ashes

An ID with no one left to ID,
spare car keys,
lost cash, a ten and a five
the buckle mark on the belt
tighten the void
as if the emptiness
will not fall.

Ashes—

In a brass box
on a white column
in a closed room—
rose light.

Fleck of Dust

In a speck of light, above a ladder,
a boy with a cowlick and a lost, helpful face
looked up to a square hole in the ceiling.

Above, a man with a beard, ponytail, cap, hammer, radial saw
cut lightly in the sawdust and cursed the humidity.

One fleck of wood-dust floated for its ever,
spinning for its ever in the sliver of light
heavier than other dust falling to the floor.

Then, the man with the beard and the smiling eyes watched
while the boy grabbed a broom.

Water and Air

Water never stops in the air
or the dry desert.

It hides in the sequoia
and in the sleeping lizards,
flowing warm, cold, moderate,
or frozen in one long in-breath

that may last twenty thousand years
for something to tap, solid,
until it can turn to the sun
and yawn its way to the bottom
of the oceans to the cracks in the mantle,
to the rivers of rock, red and molten,
to build pressure for the outbreath—

ash, lightening, the moment,
the pyroclastic cloud covers
and burns to preserve all in grey stone
then feed a new seed, a sprout, a pine,

to bring up the water,
to interpret the words of the wind.

Natural Pain

Natural wind, rock, tears of loss,
isolated ashes of one's father—

only father's day cards
in the storage room full of spiders.

Relative pain seems so individual—
leg cramps and back pain.

This current pulls one along
and bashes one's arms, legs,

mind on each jagged rock
under the illusive surface,

or it breathes enough to lay back,
float, and watch the day's light

shift from the direct summer
to the yellow slanted Autumn.

The branch, the stone, the hailstorm,
dresses in ordinary communal grieving.

The Last Gaping Yawn

Their mouths lay opened like skulls.
One man coughed like a death call, then slept.

A chant played near another of the three skeletal men.
To his left, near the white and baby-blue wall,
the more lucid man stared at us, the only moving things.

His eyes were complete, bored, mostly blank,
but they implored deeply, needing the end to come.
He waited, and he knew he was waiting.

How many brick walls did these men build
before arriving at their last beds lying unaware like bones?

Did they deliver packages? Were they ever threatened with death
by those who held the importance of power so many decades before?
What remains in those bones of the work they contributed?
Their stories, each struggle in their sunken sockets, lay with these men.

The one who watched never stopped watching.
The one who slept peacefully seemed not to breathe.
The one who slept stopped breathing,
then gurgled through a moaning yawn.
The one awake waited with eyes open.

How unimportant accumulations seem when the end
looks like the loss of memory, mind, and muscle.

In the sterile, dull-white hallway,
mysterious incense—
those waiting danced invisibly.

Glass thin Denial

The expectation that a clear, thin sheet of glass,
if walked on carefully, will not shatter
                                      cracks the glass.

Pieces would lie all around, ankle deep.

Bulbs would be yanked from the ground too soon.
Lizards would forget about window screens.
No one would eat off each other's plates.

Sharp ends would be left over,
cutting along phone lines with the tensest burdens
and in the silent corners.

Black Glass

Conflicts erode the sharp edges
we carry like black slag on newborn obsidian.

Force meets force.
Wind sings across solid ash
like gut molten angers
erupting in sparks.

I become the father and you the son,
and you, the daughter.
When I'm smoothworn grey,
smiling under paper hair,
your cliffrock corners, jagged edges
like steeples of the self that challenge the sea
will stand against the bashing water waves
until your back dissolves to sand.

Broken Bottles

Broken bottles reflect the morning dew-glass sunrise.
My attention, cut to shards, sees all pieces,
the sharp and the pleasing, unified by a waving prism
like waterbeads on blades of grass.
What was is now. Preconditions nourish
those simple illusions.

Look now. The slanted, autumn evening light
sipped by tongues of yellow leaves
overflows the tree limbs,
spills along the dried grass
and into the mouths of broken bottles,
fragments of delight and sorrow.

Brisk wind whispers for long sleeves,
a beginning, and a cold mood.
Birds' songs dip a half pitch.
Thunder shatters heat.
My boots dig deeper in the mud.
Hot tea sips cold wind.

Light like this—evening casting shadows onto morning—
twinkles from the sharpest edges of shattered glass
like soft shifting river waves,
grounds brilliance, and illuminates

broken glass that holds nothing but light.

From Now Until

From now until this time tomorrow…
        we drag our city-metal outfits
        behind us, burdened
        with the weight of that identity—
                inside us, we exchange junked heaps
                of machine-sculpted products
                for hours of folding papers
                and licking envelops—

From now until this time tomorrow…
        we promise a flat street
        that will be free to venture,
        but that stops,
                predestined by the curbs
                and rubber of our tires—
                the directions no longer
                indicated by our feet.

From now until this time tomorrow…
        we climb up dirt roads
        to seek an institute for a glimpse
        of something other—
                though we peek
                from inside brokenness
                seeing others bow
                or spin shiny, foreign paper wheels.

From now until this time tomorrow…
        we bow and spin and wonder
        if, from within our buried city selves,
                sedimentary skyscrapers
                shell us within this dream we seek.

Dead Tree and Rotting Mobile Home

Once there was shade
in the yard, off the front porch,
where that vulture sits now;
it flew away when the whitebirds
alerted in a loose V and waved
their wings on air in circles
to check if I still stood near
their roosting time.

Probably something to drink
when the tree was full and
the firewheels stared
at the sun, and some cicadas
announced the heat.

The washer shook that wall,
most likely, grinding clothes
together in soap and water
and spinning erratically
shaking the house
like an arrhythmic metal drum.

The front door holds
a faded redness for faded luck,
or to keep the demons
from knocking and asking
for obscure conversations
leading to suggested favors.

The vulture should return,
however, and wait for the door
to fade to brown, or fall face down,
then to fly in and stick its beak
into the rotting body of those memories.

The Dry, Red Desert

The dry, red valley at the edge of the desert
guards a secret below the peaks of red, bare-rock mountains
that cup the dry-brown coarse flat land
where scraggly brush scrubs the air for rare moisture.

Lizards clutch branches, visible with their clenched smirks.
Proud centurion bucks with white streaks on the breasts
show their rank, patrolling the desert foothills.

The heat stands still, gripping the air
like thirsty dry teeth that sink into the roughest scales.

Like an emerging gem, a dark smear of rain above a red peak
slides across the desert like the first stroke on a hot canvas,
painting another red pebble, one at a time, forever,
like a brush tied to the tail of a giant black tortoise
swaying right to left, weaving undulant lines
along the reddening cracked soil.

After the storm evaporates,
the desert withdraws, playing quiet,
pretending to be dry, silent, and asleep.

Our Bones

A young woman had wrapped her knee
in a black cloth brace. She said that
the weather, when the cold wind comes,
hurts her leg. The pain is core.

I said that the cold flares my emotional scars,
and turbulent storms, black swirling clouds,
make me hyper minutes before they arrive,
like deep green tea in cups upside down.

She said that her mother's bones ache
in every place they've been broken.
I did not ask how she'd broken so many bones,
or if she'd been thrown by a terrible storm.

Outside, wind sprinted to enwrap the trees,
whipping their branches around with wrestled greeting.
The cold wake of the wind slipped
into the cracks in the mind of our bones,
                                    our old storms.

The Book of Waves

You say this is the end of time
and that all is like a movie
where each moment is a photo frame
on a strip of endless film,

and you say there is no motion
and that we are the perceivers
of a clot of bundled snapshots
in which we are the subjects.

But what would time be without
the wet pages of salty waves
sliding onto shore, opening from spines,
stretching somewhere from the dark deep?

Without the gritty book cover,
particulate and portentous,
grinded by the backs of pages,
there would be no waves of sparklight.

If I should turn to walk a way
I had not been facing before,
and see the sides of beaching waves
I had not seen until I faced them,

then would it be that light rests there
if only for the time it takes
to catch my eye from where I stand
yet never to be caught again?

I see along the foamy lip
an hour of a seagull,
and depending on the rising night,
gulls mark the edge of froth lipped waves.

Like noisy words and lines that drop
between the water, sand, and air,
the line that curves and twists remains
unsnapped as waves attempt their words.

The waves leave their spit and babble,
timeless polish on tiny shells
half sunk in the grip of wet sand.
The shells clock an endless twist.
The shells curve into themselves,
endlessly speaking of timeless
pink columns of its divisions,
yet when I stoop to squeeze one shell

from the concrete grip of wet sand,
I move, the waves move, and the shell
spills birds along the ocean's waves
that slide their backs onto the shore.

The waves flow from a book spine
on the ocean floor and spread
open leaf after leaf that grinds rock to sand;
each grain reflects a spark of sun and moon.

Like crazy syntax written on the sea waves
of a never repeated sentence
in the stillest of opened books,
the pictures on a picture page

always open and never
move with the moving changes
that mark our moments with a march
of motion, sounds, and waterbirds.

Sibilant waves slide still
as if the illustration stamps timeless
on the canvas with a frenzied stillness
noiseless, static, and grey,

you say, but if this beach, the city,
these platelets of geometric timeless
events, you say, that do not move with time
in a moment when all moments stop:

the end and the beginning—one.

Coverless Night

Hands reach like tides of sleeping sand
in simple wishes of sea foam
never touching night,
not a bird near the edges
of the dream.

An under current's pull
for indefinable wants
keeps breathing and breathing
without real warmth
under limitless night's coverless light.

Who can see another's liquid soul
and believe it's not one's own?

That hand, those invisible fingers—

Ashes sink to depths no one can touch.

Cremated

Ash:
    Caramel-thick, wet, near-mud
    layers dig from the reach of the water-clear air.

Ash:
    Burned bones of the futile grasp
    of my bone-finger fist on dead pasts
    linger on the haunted present
    numbly chewing its eyes in its sockets
    of self-decomposition.

Ash:
    Too fine to be caught in perspective's filter,
    an inch thick layer per year of thoughts
    tosses moments into a blue-flamed furnace,
    their cremated bodies split to their last
    subatomic pinpoints, grey, wet layers
    of volcanic soil for the starved roots of thought.

Ash:
    Clouded days of lungs in air
    breathe of intrepid searching
    in ruined groves of wild trees.
    A spark seeks fuel
    to fill its lifetime
    with heat and light.

Ash:
    Aftermath of ideals hide on a face
    of yellowed ballots chewed by silverfish.

Ash:
    Front pages of newspapers in the fireplaces
    record pictures of saviors' tanks
    rolling over borders full of bodies
    to fulfill unattained wishes of sanctioned families.

Ash:
    Bones at the bottoms of bowl craters
    where siblings lived in cinder block walls
    clutch failed pictures in frames
    of childhood sovereignty.

Ash:
    Contrails of 30,000 feet guns
    draw new borders in the sky
    then revise them with a more accurate aim.

Ash:
    A nation eats itself
    with the spark of hunger for power
    and the fuel of week-limbed fear.

Grief and Seeking

Almost two years ago,
my father died, and it was cold
the day I looked for his car.
I assumed he drove
to the hospital for the doctors
to check his gallbladder.

I wore a thin, old, worn, black
sports coat with scuffled cuffs.
October sometimes stays warm,
but the weather aligned
with the cold of grief,
and the wind easily bit
through my jacket.

I traipsed through a blur
in each parking lot,
up and down each aisle, slowly,
looking for a short, blue car
and mistaking a few with false hope.

I asked the receptionist
if she could look up whether
he drove or that he was carried there.
She could not find the information,
so she called a security guard to help.

He pulled up in a small, enclosed cart
and invited me to sit inside.
Slowly, he drove up and down each aisle
to let me look at each car,
inside and away from the cold.

He spoke with gentle concern
and allowed me to be confused
in a warm cart next to his smile
with time enough to search
for whatever I needed to find.

Almost two years later,
(seems a day or two ago),
I finished teaching a class
and dismissed the students.

One woman held back from leaving
so that she could talk with me.
"I think my father knows you," she said,
approaching the subject with warm care.
"He is a security guard at the hospital
next to this college," she said.
"He told me he helped a teacher
look for his father's car
after his father passed away.
You are the teacher, right?"

I felt a sudden shift in time,
I felt a slight cold wind,
and I felt a warmth from a patient smile
driving me through a cold parking lot
and letting me rest within my grief.

"Oh yes!" I said. "I know him!
That was a bad day," I said.
"He helped me so much!
Please tell him thank you,
and tell him that it is still tough,
but I am doing very well."

She listened and smiled,
and I felt the day's simple kindness
as if it had never ended.

www.ingramcontent.com/pod-product-compliance
Lightning Source LLC
LaVergne TN
LVHW041552070426
835507LV00011B/1050